LINE OF FIRE

DIARY OF AN UNKNOWN SOLDIER

(AUGUST, SEPTEMBER 1914)

Thanks to the cold of winter
Thanks to Marie-Thérèse M. for her patience
Thanks to Françoise M. for his confidence
Thanks to Laetitia B. for all the research
Thanks to Frédérique G. for her uncompromising eye
Thanks to Jardin d'Alice
Thanks to all those who believed in this project

Thanks to the unknown soldier, whose diary I give you in its entirety

Barroux

LINE OF FIRE

DIARY OF AN UNKNOWN SOLDIER

(AUGUST, SEPTEMBER 1914)

BARROUX

Translated from the French
by Sarah Ardizzone

LINE OF FIRE
AN INTRODUCTION
by Michael Morpurgo

It is now a hundred years after the outbreak of the First World War, in which millions upon millions suffered and died in a holocaust of such unthinkable magnitude and such indescribable horror. It is almost impossible for us today to imagine how it must have been to live through it, to endure it. Wilfred Owen called them 'the mouthless dead'. Most were indeed 'mouthless', but some did speak out, some did tell it down in their own way. We have their witness statements. They were there.

Painters, poets and novelists; dramatists and film makers and historians have tried to tell the story, and have done it wonderfully well – and many of those were there. We have *All Quiet On The Western Front*, *Journey's End*, *Oh What A Lovely War* and *Birdsong*. We have the paintings of Paul Nash and Stanley Spencer and Christopher Nevison, and we have the poems of Owen and Sassoon and Thomas. Through these great works and many others we can have some sense of how it might have been to be there. But for me it is when the 'mouthless dead' speak directly to us, without the artifice of art, that we can best begin to understand the agony and the pity of it all; the senselessness, the waste and the futility.

In *Les Paroles des Poilus*, for instance, a collection of letters and first hand accounts, we hear the authentic voice of the soldier in the French army: a voice telling a story, not rhyming a poem, or making a story or a play, but simply speaking, telling how it was, straight. In Richard Holmes' *Tommy*, we can hear that same authentic voice, the voice of the British Tommy.

I myself, born twenty-five years after the end of the First World War, who read the poems, studied the history, watched the films and the plays, only really began to understand the horrors and terrors, the camaraderie, the humour, the sadness and the suffering, when I met someone who had been there, who had seen it all, lived it all himself. It was this chance meeting in my local pub thirty-five years ago with an old soldier - a cavalryman, a veteran of the trenches of the First World War - that convinced me I should and could write about the universality of suffering in that war, as seen through the neutral eyes of a war horse, as much a victim as any of the soldiers and civilians who died on all sides in that war.

But *War Horse* is a work of fiction: an attempt to imagine, to tell another kind of truth certainly, but nonetheless a contrived truth. It is not the voice of someone who was there, who saw it, heard it, felt it, suffered it. We need the voice of a witness to tell the unadulterated truth. We have it in this remarkable book.

It is a book of evidence. *Line of Fire* is not a work of fiction, it is a witness statement: the untrammelled, unedited voice of someone who was there. Here are the daily jottings, the notebook of an unknown soldier in the French Army, an ordinary enough man, like millions of them on all sides who finds himself born away from the normality of his everyday existence and thrust into the hideous violence of war. Here you will find no high flown prose or poetry; no sophisticated explanations, no elaboration, no embroidery or exaggeration. It is simply the written record of a man joining up and going to war, being frightened and cold and exhausted, and then wounded. It doesn't even have an end. It simply stops, as so many lives did. We don't know if this diary was lost, or if the author survived; we only know it was unsigned. We do not even know his name. All we do know is that somehow this notebook survived and was miraculously discovered.

He is the unknown soldier and these are his words.

Read them and weep.

Michael Morpurgo

I'll walk, it's not far.

I go at a steady pace from Bastille to République.
A shivery sun breaks through the clouds, winter shows its face.

The street comes to life. In front of me, two men covered in grime are huffing and puffing.

"We're emptying out the basement, help yourself, if you like!"

They tip damp papers, mouldy books, black lumps of coal and weary furniture onto the pavement.

In the middle of dusty words and smiles turned yellow with time, a cardboard box catches my eye.

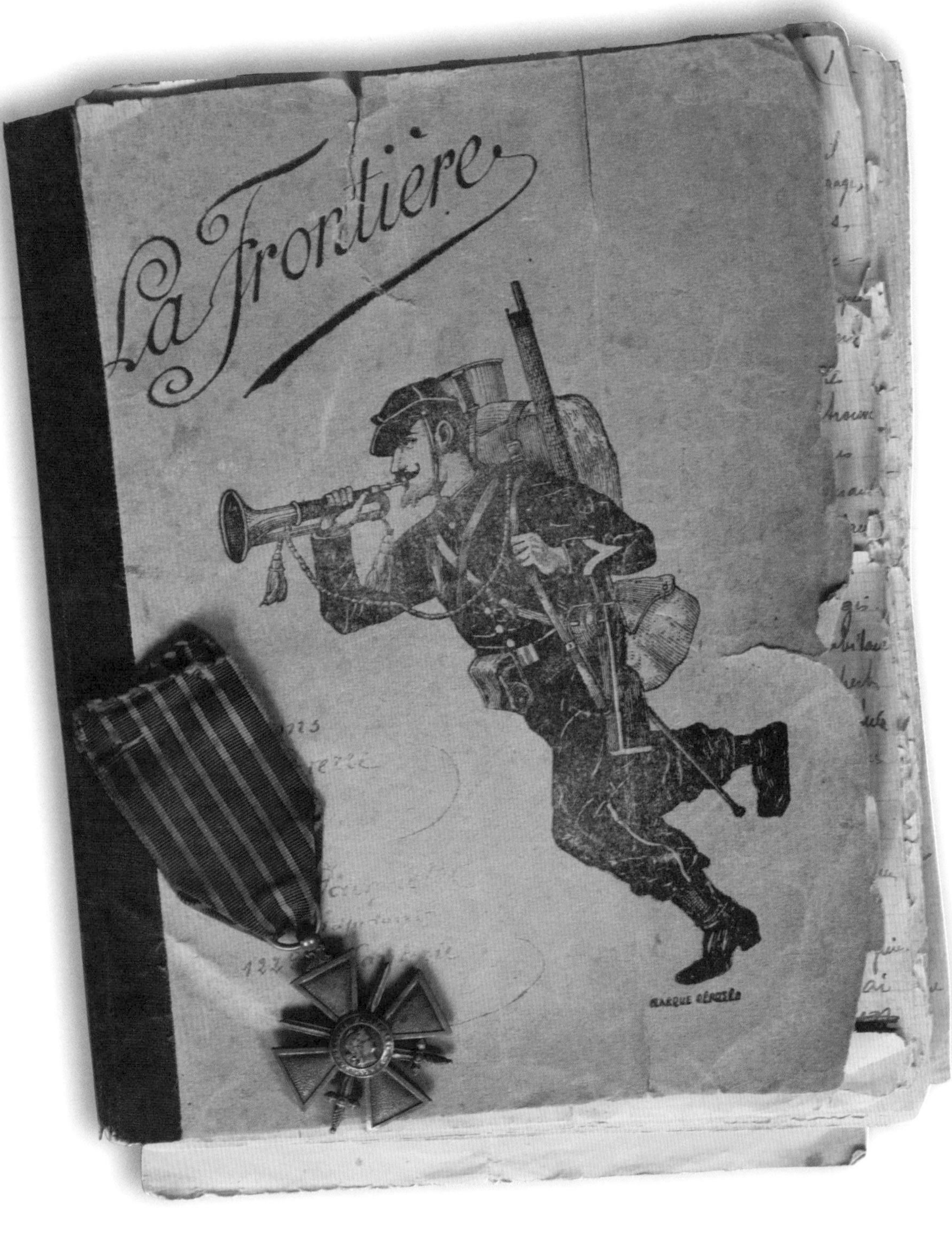
La Frontière

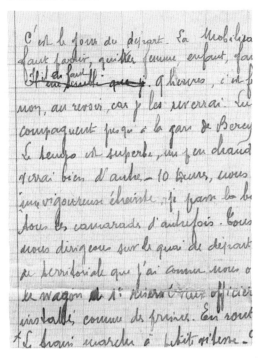

Today we're off. Mobilisation has been declared, and it's time to go, leaving behind wife, children and family. My morale is good, it has to be. 09:00 hours. This is it: farewell to all. No, goodbye. For I shall see them again.

Lucien and René accompany me to Bercy Station, where I've been summoned. The weather is glorious. A bit hot, but pleasant. I shall see others.

10:00 hours, arrival. After holding each other tight, I go through the barrier and meet up with my army friends from the old days. Everyone is in good spirits. We head for the departure platform.

There, I recognise a lieutenant from the territorial infantry who invites us to join him in the first class carriage reserved for officers, and soon we're as comfortable as princes.

What a mess inside! I collect what I need and then we go to the home of his parents-in-law. I am welcomed by Madame Fernand and her parents as if I were one of the family. These decent people are trying to ease the pain of separation in the morning.

After a wholesome dinner, I am shown to my bedroom. I fall asleep, but not without a final thought for those I've left behind.

05:00 hours: Up early as today the company has to move to its billets in town. We reach the barracks where I rush to hang up my bag and equipment.

Afterwards, during company parade in the yard, rations and ammunition are doled out.

Not being assigned to a platoon, I enlist as an extra for the 3rd, which is the sergeant-major's platoon and, more importantly, Fernand's platoon, so we'll be staying together from now on. Towards 10:00 hours, everything is ready and we leave to take up our billets while awaiting departure, which is set for the following morning.

Newspapers arrive from Paris announcing that the bad news is official. War has been declared. This is it then, we're going to fight!

How many of the soldiers we see filing past will make it safely back to their homes? Let us banish dark thoughts and take heart again.

The women weep. It's up to us to show them we're stronger than they are and convince them we will return.

But we have to report back to our companies, where the afternoon will be taken up with inspections by the captain and the major. It's imperative that every man be in position and that nothing is missing. At last, everything is ready. We return to the house.

After dinner I go to see Maurice, whom I've always held in high respect. He tries to cheer me up by saying that war isn't as bloody as people think. May his words be true! When I take my leave, he says how sorry he is not to be coming with us. The evening winds to a sad close and I make for my bedroom, giving thanks for these good people who have softened the blow of the first two days of separation.

WEDNESDAY 5 AUGUST

This time, it's the great send-off. We're up at 04:00 hours because parade is at 05:00 hours. After collecting our haversacks filled with bread and a rabbit cooked the previous day, it's time for farewells.

All five of us shed a tear. After promising Madame Fernand that we'll stick together, we leave with heavy hearts, but our sense of duty makes us hold our heads high and soon we've joined the ranks, ready for the off.

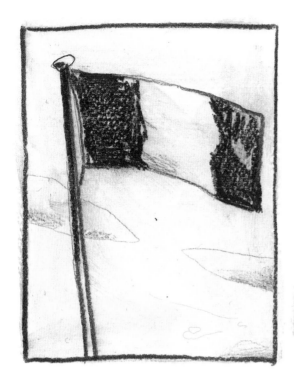

Once the regiment is on parade, the colonel has us salute the flag and he gives a rousing speech, which is met with cheers. Then we march to the station with the band playing.

07:00 hours: The train whistles and sets off in the direction of Paris. What a cruel irony! After a stop at Corbeil, the train departs again but this time heading eastwards. At the stations, the ladies from the Red Cross bring us food and drink. We pass though Montereau, Romilly and Troyes. Where are we going? Who knows.

I try to sleep, but to no avail. My lower back is going numb. Two o'clock in the morning. Bar-Le-Duc. When will we stop?

THURSDAY 6 AUGUST

05:00 hours: We de-train at Lebeuville in the morning rain. After a halt of an hour, during which we make coffee, we move off again. Slowly but surely, the sun rises and begins to warm us. My feet hurt. I'm off to a good start!

We arrive within view of Saint-Mihiel and make a longer stop. I overhear a conversation between the major and the officer, to the effect that we'll probably stay here for a few days. I take this opportunity to forward my address.

We cross the town and reach our billet, which is the barracks of the 25th Battalion of Light Infantry. I'm starting to hobble. Everything is untidy, suggesting a hasty departure. The beds are unmade and kits are strewn across the floor. You'd think the battalion was just out on an exercise or a route march.

At last, we'll be able to rest up from the journey. There are beds for everyone. I take off my socks and notice that my feet are covered in blisters. I'm dreading our next marches.

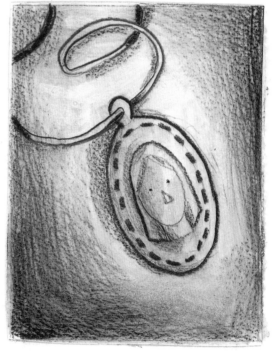

On opening my bag, I find a lucky charm hidden by my dear wife and a tear comes to my eye.

After washing from head to toe, Fernand and I go to visit the 40th Artillery Regiment opposite. Here, the same shambles, as well as some ladies of questionable morals loitering about the buildings under the pretext of cleaning, although I suspect with an altogether different purpose.

Disgusted, we leave and head into town on the hunt for supper. After much searching, we track down a bowl of broth and some steak with chips at a wine merchant's. 20:00 hours, we return and go to bed.

From 05:00 hours, the battalion falls in. Our stay is already over. We move off in an eastwards direction. It's hot, the roads are hard and my feet hurt. Towards 08:00 hours, we reach Buissières, where an ambulance outside the town hall gives us a foretaste of battle.

Fernand finds us a good bottle of wine, which goes some way towards cheering us up. After quite a long halt in the square, we spread out along a small railway track where we must dig trenches behind the embankments. Suddenly, a storm bursts and we bear the brunt of it on our backs.

Once the rain has stopped, we head back into town to join our billets. The sergeant-major has found a small bedroom in a deserted house and, with some straw, it's fit for a king. No news from Paris yet. Time is starting to drag.

SATURDAY 08 AUGUST

From 05:00 hours, we set out again to work on the trenches. We're beginning to hear the sound of artillery fire in the distance.

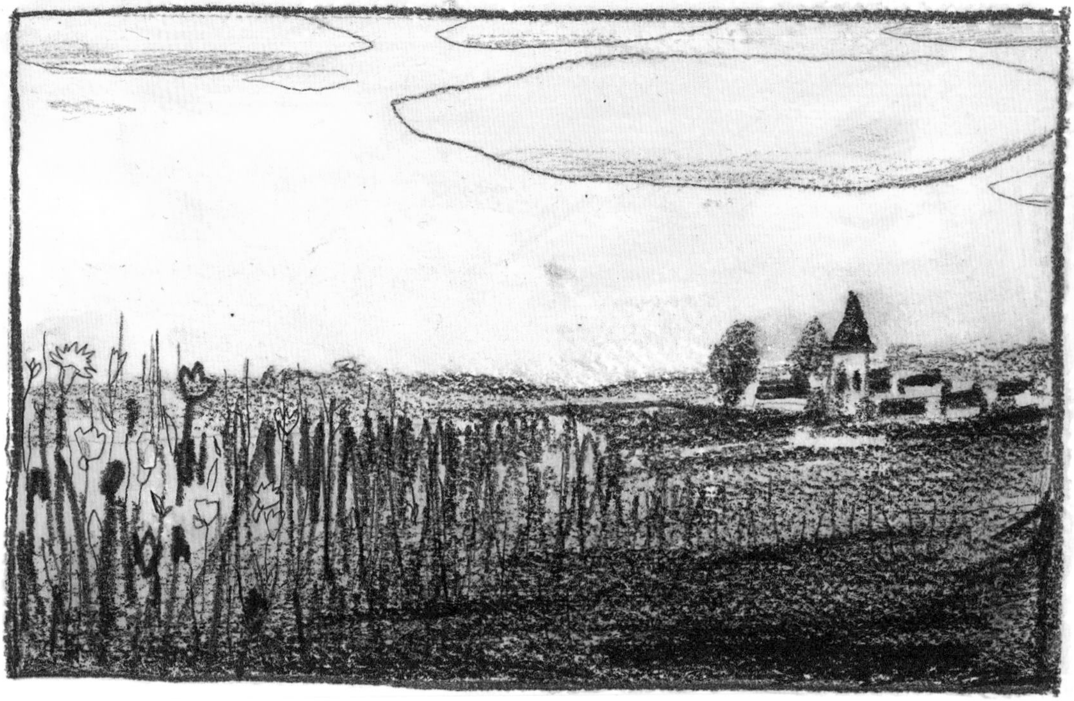

At midday, I return to the village with a squad charged with resting up prior to mounting the night guard. I note our instructions and go to examine the sector I'm to watch. Then I take a stroll around. Nothing of any interest. Evening comes, the company returns and it's time to eat.

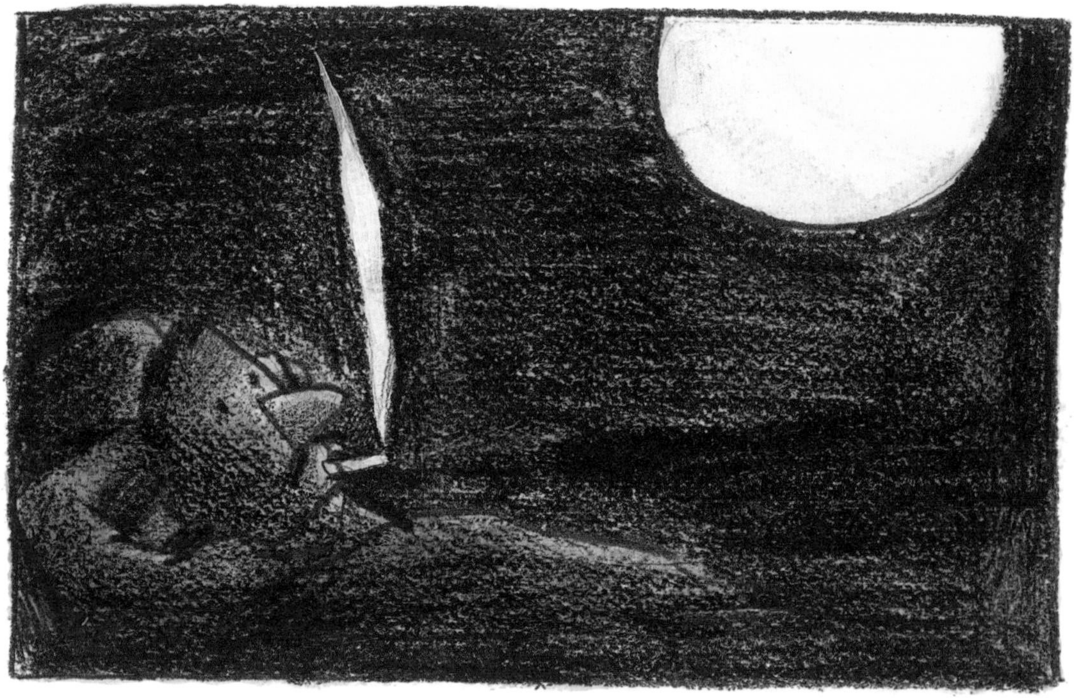

The fires die down and everyone falls asleep. In the moonlight I dream of those I've left behind and of whom I still have no news. My heart grows heavy and so as not to dwell on things, I take a turn round my patch, before heading back to lie on the straw. The night draws to a close without incident.

A glorious sunrise, it's going to be a hot day. We leave for the trenches. May we stay here for a long time! We can still hear the distant rumbling of artillery fire. At midday, the order for us to depart comes at the same time as the news that Mulhouse has been captured by the French.

We set off with happy hearts, as the locals wish us good luck. The heat is sweltering and it's uphill all the way. We arrive at nightfall. Everybody is exhausted: officers and men alike.

We halt before entering the commune. Are we going to be billeted here? But no, we take to the road again and march further through a night as black as ink. We're heading in the direction of Verdun. When are we going to stop?

My feet are bleeding. My legs can no longer hold me up. This isn't a man who's walking, but a sheep following the flock. Fernand is as tired as I am.

At last, we reach a village as the clock strikes two. Accommodation is in short supply. It's impossible to house everybody. So Fernand and I are back on the road, without shelter, and scarcely able to put one foot in front of the other.

In the end we manage to find a barn occupied by only two gunners and, after talking it over, we share their straw and lie down. Phew!

By 05:00 hours we have to be off again. I'm all done in, but the captain confirms we're not going far. Sure enough, towards 08:00 hours we reach the entrance to Ancemont, home to senator Charles Humbert, whose property we catch sight of.

We enjoy good quarters here with a woman whose husband is at Verdun. Also with her in the house are her mother and sister, forced to evacuate Verdun. We'll be able to wash and rest up while awaiting our departure orders, perhaps in the night.

At 05:00 hours, parade, but we're not leaving. The men clean their weapons. In short, this is a rest day. Suddenly, there's an announcement that letters have arrived. I rush over, and there are two for me, but dated the 3rd and 4th. They don't tell me anything new.

Still, it does us good to read news that has reached us from far away. While we're eating, the sergeant-major tasks me with finding a rabbit for the following day. I fall asleep happy to have received some news.

Parade at 05:00 hours, but still no order to move. I take care of the cooking, having found a decent rabbit which I stew with potatoes. It'll last us the day.

In the evening, after we've eaten, we smoke cigarettes in the garden and a man from the platoon, Simon de Rebbars, once a café-concert artist, sings us some light-hearted ditties. You really wouldn't think we were at war.

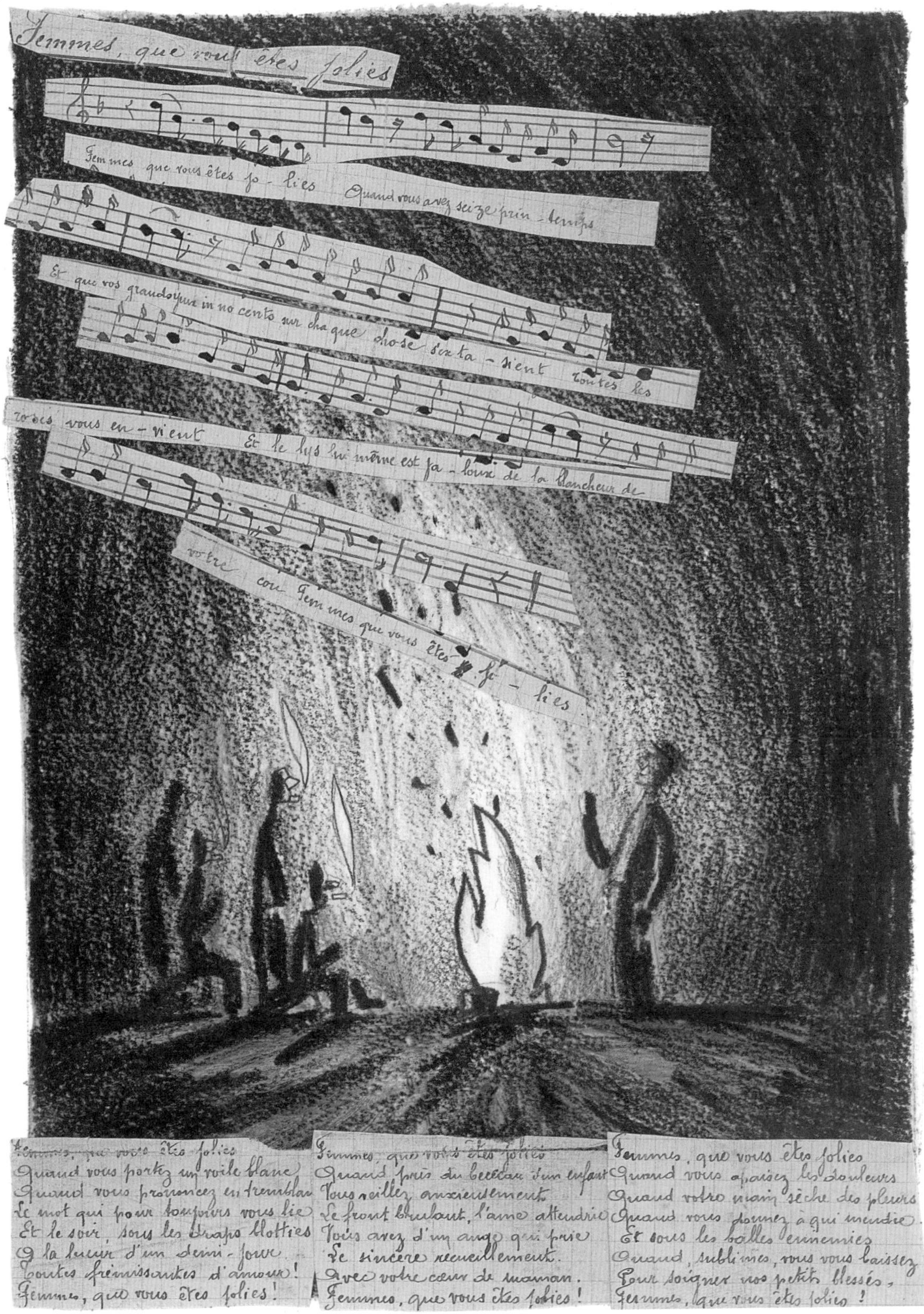
Femmes, que vous êtes jolies
Femmes que vous êtes jo - lies
Quand vous avez seize prin - temps
Et que vos grands yeux in no cents sur chaque chose sex ta - sient toutes les
roses vous en - vient
Et le lys lui même est ja - loux de la blancheur de
votre cou
Femmes que vous êtes jo - lies
Femmes, que vous êtes jolies
Quand vous portez un voile blanc
Quand vous prononcez en tremblan
Le mot qui pour toujours vous lie
Et le soir, sous les draps blotties
A la lueur d'un demi-jour
Toutes frémissantes d'amour!
Femmes, que vous êtes jolies!
Femmes que vous êtes jolies
Quand près du berceau d'un enfant
Vous veillez anxieusement
Le front brûlant, l'âme attendrie
Vous avez d'un ange qui prie
Le sincère recueillement
Avec votre cœur de maman.
Femmes, que vous êtes jolies!
Femmes, que vous êtes jolies
Quand vous apaisez les douleurs
Quand votre main sèche des pleurs
Quand vous donnez à qui mendie
Et sous les balles ennemies
Quand, sublimes, vous vous baissez
Pour soigner nos petits blessés,
Femmes, que vous êtes jolies!

Still no order to move on. The captain decides to make us do some exercises. This gets us through the morning, but the afternoon drags on.

At last, evening comes and we lie down, but no one can sleep in the barn and so jokes fly back and forth. This goes on until nearly 11 o'clock. At midnight, a wake-up call. This time we're off and sad to be leaving Ancemont, taking with us the memory of a good stay.

After skirting around Verdun, we head northwards and march until midday in sweltering heat.

I find a stick and use it to support my aching feet. I can use it to fly the platoon's colours. As soon as darkness falls, no one needs any encouragement to lie down on the straw.

As soon as I'm up, I set off in search of a duck for lunch. Our base is now a meadow and we enjoy a very successful meal in the open air.

Supper is equally pleasant, although wine is getting hard to find. Still no news, the situation is becoming worrying.

The captain has bought a pig for the company. It's the first time I've seen a pig slaughtered and butchered. The NCOs of the 3rd section take their share. Our cook prepares a succulent roast.

Another tasty picnic but washed down with water, the wine being notable for its absence. This evening, the same menu, and the day draws to a close without me receiving any more news.

Will we stay here much longer? The 4th Infantry Regiment is 3km ahead of us, while the rest of the regiment, which was behind us, is coming to occupy the area. The day passes without incident.

TUESDAY 18 AUGUST

We set off first thing in the morning to occupy Grémilly, 3km away, in order to replace the 4th Regiment which is moving on to Azannes. This is meant to be our final station. The announcement comes that the Prussians are barely 14km ahead of us. We're starting to feel like we're at war. Still no news.

We march through fields surrounding the village. In the afternoon, the captain carries out an inspection. You'd think we were back at the barracks.

THURSDAY 20 AUGUST

The same again: exercises in the morning, inspection in the afternoon. I didn't expect to see this in wartime. It's becoming tedious. Still no news for me. I feel low. Then comes the announcement that the Prussians have destroyed the village of Pillon 10km ahead of us, before retreating.

At 05:30 hours, we set off in the direction of Longwy. We pass through Anzannes and Mangiennes, where a battle took place a few days earlier.

By the side of the road, a pair of modest crosses marks the spot where two soldiers died.

Everywhere in the fields, we can see the shell cases left behind by the gunners. It's starting to smell of war. After passing Longwy, where the residents cheer and hand out drinks, the captain tells us that our vanguard has come into contact with the enemy around Longwy.

Towards 17:00 hours, the sound of artillery fire can be heard more clearly. The battalion deploys in a field and we take up our defence positions against the artillery.

We've covered more than 40km and everybody slumps to the ground for a break. I'm drenched in sweat. All of a sudden, the sky turns black and a violent storm breaks.

No chance of shelter. We're soaked to the bone.

At last, we reach Beaumont as night falls. Fernand finds a house with a good fire and I join him to dry off.

But someone comes to tell Fernand that he and his half-platoon must stand guard duty at the exits to the village, and so we move off into the night.

We discover the most hospitable of houses

where the owner plies us with coffee and brandy to help us through the night. He even offers us a bed, but we can't take him up on it, being on guard duty and subject to a night alert.

I take a turn outside for a moment, it's pitch black, the artillery has stopped rumbling. In the distance, two villages set alight by the Prussians spread their reddish glow through the darkness. Sickened, I go back inside and lie down for a while on the straw.

At dawn, the gunfire begins its song again. The regiment deploys, and we are the reserve for the army corps. We can hear the sound of gunfire clearly now. There's a wood in front of us, out of which soon emerge the wounded from the regiments in battle ahead of us.

Some drag a leg, others have sustained injuries to the arm or head. Two battalions have already passed through these woods and soon it will be our turn.

The noise is deafening. Our battalion receives the order to occupy Saint-Rémy, a Belgian village on the border about 2km away from these woods. And so we find ourselves rushing down a slope, before advancing in successive dashes at the bottom of a basin over which the German shrapnel rages.

From time to time the barbed wire stops us, but we're still making progress. The sun is directly overhead, so it must be midday or thereabouts. But nobody is thinking about the heat or how tired he is.

At last, we arrive at Saint-Rémy, but there's not a soul in the village. We do a headcount: no one wounded, no one dead. Come on, the German artillery isn't that lethal after all!

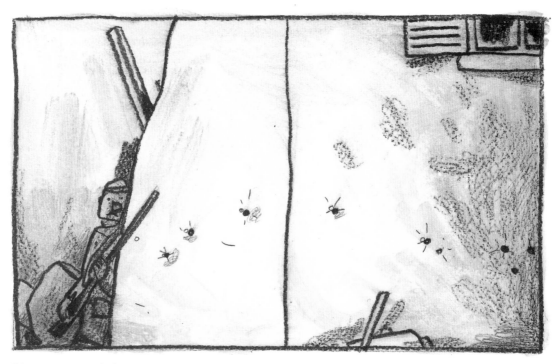

We can see our infantry ahead of us fighting every step of the way and, further off, the German infantry whose bullets are beginning to reach us. An order comes to withdraw.

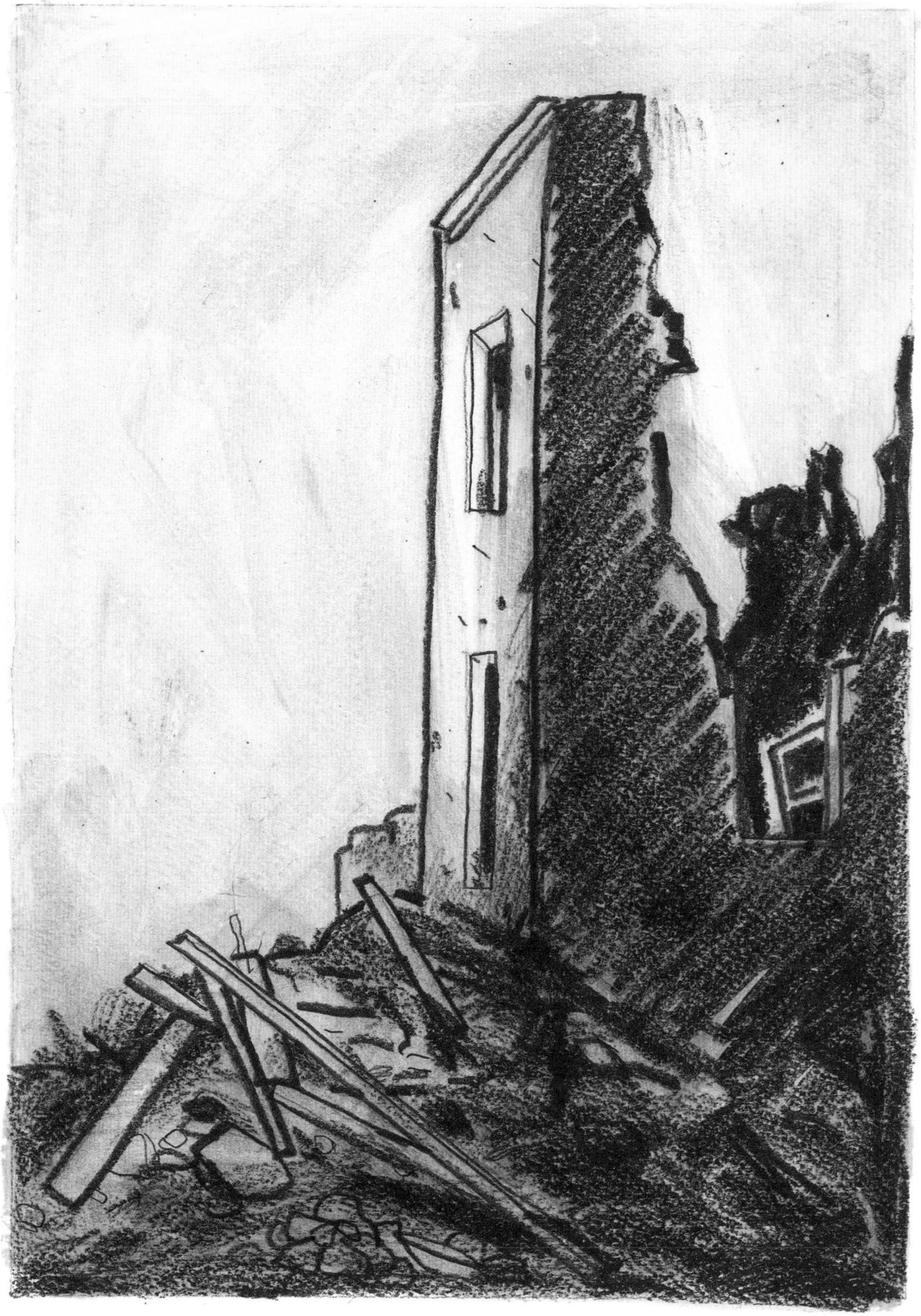

The company has to climb a ridge that's at least 300 metres high. We begin our ascent with successive dashes, but shells follow each dash and this time they're powerful, carving out holes around us big enough to bury a horse.

The captain keeps advancing, followed only by a few men including Fernand and me. The rest are scattered across the ridge. A few hide behind wheatsheaves, in the belief this will shelter them.

More and more shells are raining down. At last we reach the top of the ridge, before descending the other side at top speed. Now the captain has nothing left around him apart from the 3rd platoon and a few isolated men from the other platoons.

We set off to join the muster spot, where the regiment behind us is gathering. But it's still a long way off and I'm all done in. We rejoin the Longwy road, which is clogged with carts and trucks full of the wounded.

Retreating groups from every regiment pass by. This is a rout: we are in retreat. I'm forced to leave the column because I can no longer put one foot in front of the other.

I lean on my stick and Fernand stays with me. He is as tired as I am. Still, we've had a lucky escape. At last, we catch up with the regiment, which has stopped in a field.

Little by little, the companies are reunited and we retreat still further back. It's dark by the time we reach a cornfield where we make an overnight camp.

We find some straw and Fernand and I lie down, side by side to keep each other warm. I don't waste any time closing my eyes.

The cold wakes me at dawn. In any event, we have to be off and digging trenches. A short rest gives us a chance to make some food.

The artillery thunders and seems to be getting ever closer. Sure enough, we've barely had time to eat when ahead of us we notice the smoke from the exploding shells. We have to withdraw again.

Once on the road, we overtake civilians fleeing the Prussian invasion and it's harrowing to see these wagons filled with women and children who've had to abandon their homes, while the father is doing his duty in the army.

After passing through deserted villages we take up position in open country, behind an oat field where we start digging trenches again.

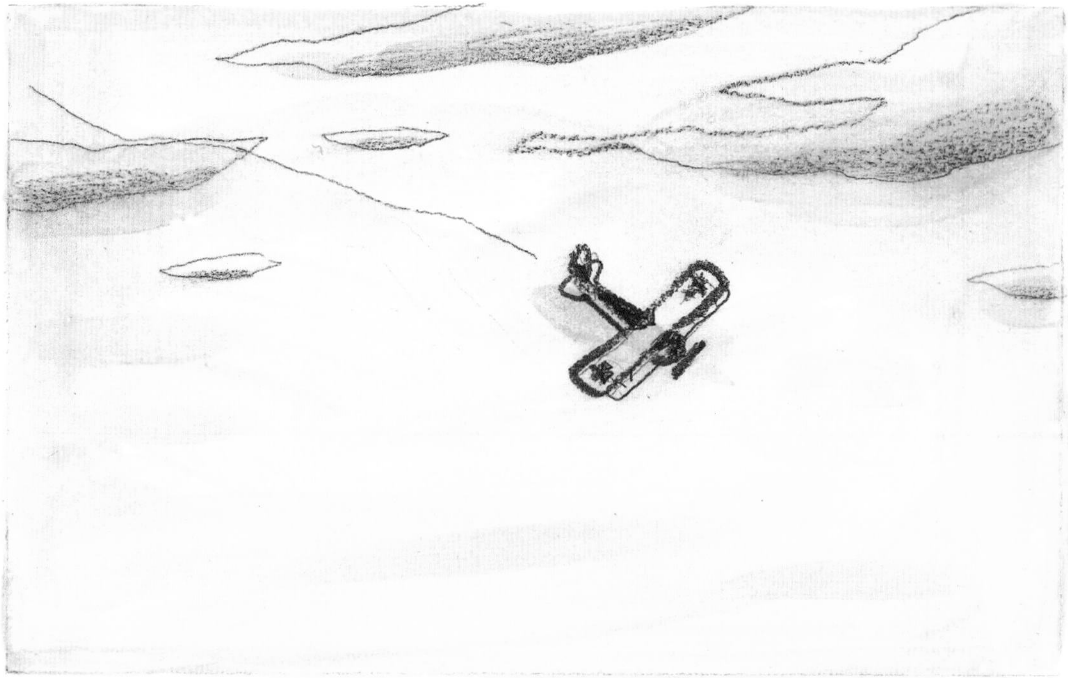

Soon a roaring overhead signals a German aeroplane. It has barely disappeared on the horizon when the German artillery, informed by it, begins to fire shells at us.

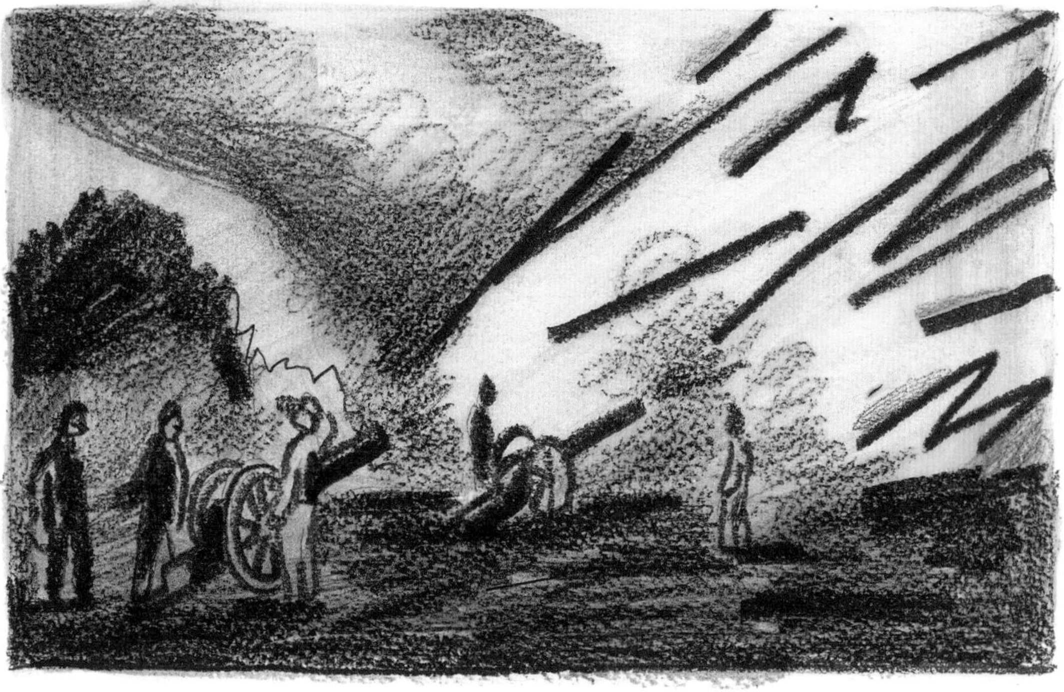

But our artillery responds, and until nightfall there is a deafening noise.

When night finally comes we make camp, but the 3rd platoon is dispatched to take up position at the edge of the forest and, this time, it will be a sleepless night.

The red from the fires still glimmers in the distance.

Somehow, we make it through the night. I struggle against drowsiness and exhaustion. Daylight at last and the cool of morning wakes me. But from the woods, a cry goes up: "Ow, my arm!"

It's a wounded man who has spent the whole night not knowing whether he was surrounded by French or Prussians. The stretcher-bearers carry him off while we resume our places in yesterday's trenches.

But the gunfire rages and soon we have to withdraw. After a roundabout route, we reach the forest at Marville towards the end of the day, where we begin digging trenches into the hillside, opposite a ridge which the German artillery wastes no time in shelling.

But night comes and we stay in our trenches.

At first light, the aeroplane carries out its reconnaissance and soon the shells start raining down. We leave and must cross a forest where the paths are unfit for our purpose.

Forced to march in single file, our column stretches out as the German artillery begins to attack the woods. Will we get out of here alive? After many a nerve-wracking moment, the company emerges intact on the other side. No doubt about it, we've been very lucky.

We go through deserted villages. It's pitiful to think that soon the Prussians will turn up and wreak bloody havoc.

We keep marching, I am exhausted and haunted by one thought: rest. Eventually, we stop in view of a village, which is Peuvillers. The battalion is deployed in front of the village and we start digging trenches again.

Towards evening, an aeroplane passes overhead. It is flying low and we spot a French pilot, at last!

WEDNESDAY 26 AUGUST

The night doesn't last long. It is perhaps midnight when we're woken. We must leave. So when will we stop? After some thirty kilometres, we reach the banks of the Meuse.

The Meuse: which we need to cross tonight. But before then the battalion must provide the rearguard for the army corps, remaining on the high ground opposite the enemy, as we've been informed that their cavalry is making reconnaissance patrols. And indeed, from time to time a figure appears on the horizon.

The 3rd platoon is dispatched to the canal to ensure we maintain contact with the troops to our right. Will we spend the night here? It's chilly. A light drizzle does nothing to warm us up.

As evening sets in a cyclist arrives with instructions for us to reach the village of Vilosnes, where we'll find the bridge we must cross and blow up under the cover of darkness. He tells us that all the other troops have crossed the Meuse and that we are the only ones left on this side.

Just then, an explosion is heard. Is it the bridge? Are we ready? The platoon moves at the double and, despite our fatigue, there are no laggards. We quickly cover the 500 metres separating us from the bridge. Phew! It's still there. It was just a footbridge that got blown up!

We cross the Meuse with a great sense of relief. Then we set off into the darkness again. We reach Nantillois in the pouring rain, at 11 o'clock in the evening, only to learn that the place is already occupied by our soldiers and we can't be billeted.

It's each for himself when it comes to finding a spot in a barn. I take Fernand with me and we go looking for somewhere to shelter the two of us. We find a ladder propped against a wall, next to an open window.

I climb up to explore inside the house, and find myself in an empty bedroom containing sacks and straw. I call out to Fernand who joins me, and we begin to make ourselves comfortable.

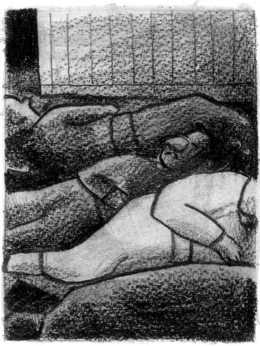

But soon, our quarters are invaded by an avalanche of soldiers on the quest for a roof over their heads. Happily, there's room for everybody and I lie down on the straw, snug inside a sack.

Not until 10:00 hours do we leave to occupy more habitable quarters. We reach Cunel after 5km, where we can rest for a whole day. I still haven't received any news and I am truly worried.

FRIDAY 28 AUGUST

From 05:00 hours, the 3rd platoon is instructed to mount guard and leaves to take up its station. It's a long day, but at least we don't hear the sound of the artillery. The companies have gone to dig trenches around the commune, and everything is calm.

Evening comes and at last I receive some postcards from my dear wife, dated the 19th-22nd. The news is good, and my spirits are raised a little.

As for the night, it's impossible to sleep in the barn, which is being used as a command post, so I lie down next to Fernand on a wagon where we've spread some straw.

The cold of darkness wakes me well before daybreak.

The shift is relieved and our platoon rejoins the company. After a march under trees we return to take up our position by the clearing, where we remain until evening while the sound of gunfire rumbles away.

Several German planes fly overhead, but we're well hidden. At nightfall we return to our camp and, after a decent coffee, I get ready for a good night.

But towards 10:00 hours, we get our wake-up call. The company must go to Aincreville to make contact with the 4th army corps. After a two-hour march through the night, we arrive and I can sleep for a few hours.

We move behind the 4th corps, but the German artillery is raging and we have to withdraw back to Aincreville again.

Evening catches us near a small stream that borders the area, as deafening shells fall on the village and around us, carving huge craters.

Under the cover of darkness, we return to Cunel without a single man injured. But upon arrival, we're directed to the road flanking the wood we occupied yesterday.

And it's in a field that we will have to spend the night.

At dawn, we set off in the direction of Dun-sur-Meuse. Skirting the forest, I notice a soldier's leg hanging from a branch. This is where a powerful shell landed on a platoon of the 6th company, which was partially destroyed.

We take up our positions behind a ridge to the sound of artillery fire. We make slow progress and, after crossing a road, we occupy the crest in the middle of an oat field.

But soon the shrapnel erupts overhead and we must advance.

As I stand up, a pain in my left arm stops me. I push up my sleeve and see a hole in my arm, with blood pouring out.

Quickly, I remove my field dressing from my pocket and hold it out to a nearby soldier, for him to treat me. While he's bandaging my arm, the shells continue to rain down around us.

I shall never forget the devotion of this soldier who didn't think twice about risking his life, staying close in order to tend to me. The artillery rumbles. We wish each other good luck as we part ways, and I return to the road by crawling on my belly.

The shrapnel is still exploding above me and I experience a moment of indescribable panic.

At last, it's the road! I throw myself into the ditch and follow it, as quickly as I can. I encounter some stragglers, including one who offers to accompany me and carry my bag. I'm so exhausted that I don't have the strength to refuse and we continue on our way.

But my arm is causing me a lot of pain and the first village is still a way off. We stop by the roadside and, on the basis that I probably have a fracture, I get my companion to cut a branch lengthways, and help me attach these splints on either side of my arm.

We set off for Bantheville where, several turns later, we eventually find an ambulance and I climb onboard. Phew! I'm all done in.

Having picked up three other wounded, we leave for Clermont-en-Argonne station where, after being jolted about on a winding road, we arrive at about 18:00 hours.

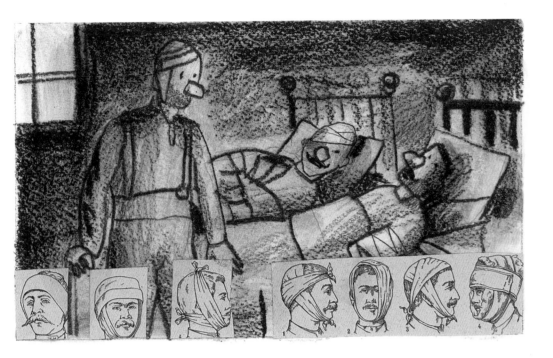

Once I've been examined by a medical officer, I go to the town hospital to be bandaged up. It's a ghastly spectacle: only the seriously wounded are kept there. Some have lost an arm, others a leg,

while a gunner who had been begging to die since the morning breathes his last.

A passing medical officer lets it be known that he has just finished his eleventh operation. No one really has time to look after me.

Still, I manage to find a male nurse who is a medical student. After removing my bandage which was applied on the battlefield, he diagnoses a fractured radius and dresses my arm as a result.

I return to the station where countless wounded are waiting for the train. I haven't eaten anything since morning, but I'm not hungry and make do with a mess tin of broth offered to me by a male nurse.

At 20:00 hours the train pulls in and I climb into the 1st class compartment with three other wounded men from the 82nd. The train sets off and I fall asleep.

After travelling all night, we reach Châlons where we have to change trains before setting off for Troyes, arriving at 10 o'clock.

Are we going to stay here? We're bundled into a barn already containing a large number of injured men. I take a moment to let my wife know I am wounded.

Bowls of broth are distributed and at 2 o'clock we catch another train, which will take us to Cahors. We wait until 4 o'clock for the train to fill up. The heat is oppressive and my arm is starting to give me grief.

At last we set off. At every station, people bring us fruit, chocolate and coffee. But it's impossible to eat anything because I've got a raging fever.

We reach Laroche and, unable to hold out any longer, I go to find the medical officer travelling with us and beg him to give me something for my fever. He tells me that the stop here isn't long enough, and that he'll organise for me to get off the train at the next station.

We reach Auxerre towards half past eight. I leave the train and climb into the ambulance, which takes me to the military hospital where I arrive in a daze at around 9 o'clock.

I locate a medical officer who changes my bandage. To my great astonishment, he informs me that the Germans are at Compiègne and getting closer to Paris every day.

I lie down in a decent bed where I fall into a deep sleep.

I awake after a good night's rest to a bowl of steaming coffee. What a turn of events! I write to my dear wife to reassure her and send her my address. At around 10 o'clock, the medical officer does his rounds.

At 11 o'clock, I am brought lunch which consists of a can of milk. It's not much, but since my fever has fallen, I'll be allowed a little meat and some potato purée in the evening.

Towards 3 o'clock, I am bandaged by the matron. A woman of staunch devotion, she does everything around here. In the daytime, some ladies pay us a visit and bring sweets.

And the evening settles in without the day seeming too long. That said, I hope to get up tomorrow.

I manage to get up today, but the time goes slowly. I get to know my companions in misfortune, including some from Paris. In particular, I strike up a friendship with a sergeant from the 19th Battalion Light Infantry, who was injured by shrapnel above his right shoulder blade.

More wounded men arrive in the evening. By 8 o'clock, I'm in bed and I drift off to sleep thinking that perhaps the Germans are in Paris.

Life in hospital is monotonous. I still haven't received any news, but I find some consolation in the fact that my dear wife must know I'm safe from the bullets.

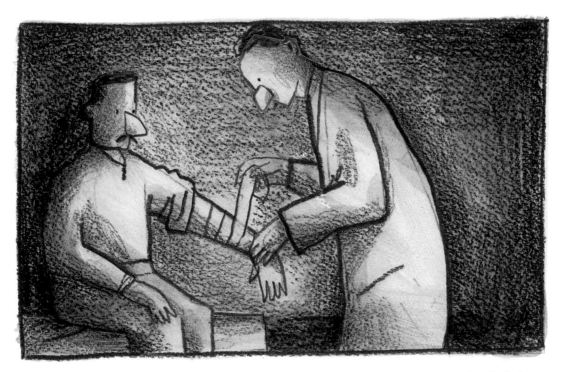

I feel wretched only having the use of one arm and frequently relying on someone else for help.

I receive a letter from Paris. Everybody is well. I would be glad to know the Germans were a little further away from those I hold dear.

SATURDAY 12 SEPTEMBER

This week seems to have gone on forever.

Life carries on just the same. I am bored to death and my heart is heavy.

Sometimes I'm sorry I didn't stay in the line of fire.

The diary found by Barroux stops here, although an accompanying notebook of songs found with the diary carries on until May 1917. We will probably never know why our soldier stopped writing his diary, or what became of him.

By chance, a curious artist out for a stroll came across these notebooks and rescued them from being destroyed. They provide us with the story of the first months of a war everybody thought would be over by Christmas, but which lasted more than four years. All this happened one hundred years ago.

air. alsace lorraine

La Question du Jour

I

Depuis deux ans que la guerre est commencée
Ce que l'on fait, tout de suite, en s'abordant
C'est de se dire d'une voix angoissée
"Crois-tu que la guerre va durer encor longtemps ?
"C'est que ça commence à devenir long tout de même
"Ah ! ce qu'on s'embête ! On serait peut-être mieux au front
"Mais je suis trop vieux — "Moi ! J'ai de l'emphysème."
"Mais je crois cependant que c'est nous qui les aurons
"Nous reprendrons l'alsace et la Lorraine.
"Y aura plus de Boches ! Y aura plus que des França
"Un officier m'a dit l'autre semaine,
"que ça s'rait p't'être fini pour le mois de Mai —

II

Pour le mois de Mai — Hélas ! avec ces drogues
Ne crois-tu pas que ça durera plus longtemps ?
Et c'est toujours, partout, le même dialogue,
Vous avouerez, qu'à la fin, c'est embêtant !
Chez mon coiffeur, cependant qu'il me rase,
En me tenant le nez, il se croit obligé,
De me répéter, à son tour, cette phrase
"Croyez-vous que les Boches seront délogés

Quand reprendrons-nous l'Alsace et la Lorraine?
Ce jour-là, Monsieur, croyez-vous, quel succès!
Et, plein d'ardeur, mon barbier, qui se démène,
Me coupe la gueule, et verse le sang français.

III

Donc, excédé, un matin, plein d'audace
Je me suis souvenu que Joffre est mon ami,
Et je suis parti, par la gare Montparnasse
Pour une bonne fois, me renseigner auprès de lui.

J'arrive là-bas à --- (Je ne puis pas le dire)
Mettons à --- X --- et Joffre me reçoit
Je lui dis ce que je veux, alors il se met à rire,
Et me dit: "Mon cher, je crois que tu te fous de moi!

"Qu'est-ce que tu me chantes avec l'Alsace-Lorraine?
"Parle-moi des pièces que l'on joue aux Français,
"Mais, de la guerre, mon vieux, c'est pas la peine:
"Je suis le seul qui n'en parle jamais."

For more information about *Line of Fire* and
the making of this book, including an online glossary,
downloadable teaching resources and translator's notes, visit:

www.lineoffirebook.com

Supported using public funding by
ARTS COUNCIL
ENGLAND

LOTTERY FUNDED

Line of Fire: Diary of an Unknown Soldier – August, September 1914
ISBN: 978-1-907912-39-9

Originally published in French in 2011 under the title *On les Aura!* by Editions du Seuil
First published in English Phoenix Yard Books Ltd, 2014

Phoenix Yard Books
Phoenix Yard
65 King's Cross Road
London
WC1X 9LW

Copyright © Editions du Seuil, 2011
English translation copyright © Sarah Ardizzone, 2014

3 5 7 9 10 8 6 4 2

A CIP catalogue record for this book is available from the British Library
Printed in Malaysia

www.phoenixyardbooks.com